Dr. Jaerock Lee

MY FATHER WILL GIVE TO YOU IN MY NAME

> *"Truly, truly, I say to you,*
> *if you ask the Father for anything in My name,*
> *He will give it to you.*
> *Until now you have asked for nothing in My name;*
> *ask and you will receive,*
> *so that your joy may be made full."*
>
> (John 16:23-24)

MY FATHER WILL GIVE TO YOU IN MY NAME by Dr. Jaerock Lee
Published by Urim Books (Representative: Kyungtae Noh)
73, Yeouidaebang-ro 22-gil, Dongjak-Gu, Seoul, Korea
www.urimbooks.com

All rights reserved. This book or parts thereof may not be reproduced in any form, stored in a retrieval system, or transmitted in any form or by any means, electronic, mechanical, photocopying, recording or otherwise, without prior written permission of the publisher.

Unless otherwise noted, all Scripture quotations are taken from the Holy Bible, NEW AMERICAN STANDARD BIBLE, ®, Copyright © 1960, 1962, 1963, 1968, 1971, 1972, 1973, 1975, 1977, 1995 by The Lockman Foundation. Used by permission.

Copyright © 2011 by Dr. Jaerock Lee
ISBN: 978-89-7557-205-0, ISBN: 978-89-7557-060-5(set)
Translation Copyright © 2009 by Dr. Esther K. Chung. Used by permission.

Previously published into Korean by Urim Books in 1990

First Published February 2009
Second Edition August 2011

Edited by Dr. Geumsun Vin
Designed by Editorial Bureau of Urim Books
Printed by Yewon Printing Company
For more information, please contact at urimbook@hotmail

A Message on Publication

"Truly, truly, I say to you, if you ask the Father for anything in My name, He will give it to you"
(John 16:23).

Christianity is a faith in which people meet the living God and experience His work through Jesus Christ.

For God is an almighty God who created the heavens and the earth and governs the history of the universe as well as life, death, curse, and blessing of man, He answers His children's prayer and desires them to lead blessed lives proper for children of God.

Anyone who is a true child of God carries with him the authority to which he is entitled as a child of God. By this authority, he ought to live a life in which all things are possible, find that he lacks nothing, and enjoy blessings without any cause to harbor envy or jealousy against others. By leading a life of overflowing affluence, strength, and success, he must give glory to God through his life.

In order to enjoy such a blessed life, one must thoroughly understand the law of the spiritual realm on God's answers and receive everything for which he asks God in the name of Jesus Christ.

This work is a compilation of messages that were preached in the past for all believers, especially those who beyond doubt believe in the almighty God and desire to lead lives full of God's answers.

May this work *My Father Will Give to You in My Name* serve as a guidebook that leads all readers to become aware of the law of the spiritual realm on God's answers and enables them to receive everything they ask for in prayer, in the name of Jesus Christ I pray!

I give all thanks and glory to God for allowing this book

carrying His precious Word to be published and express my sincere gratitude to all those who have worked arduously for this endeavor.

Jaerock Lee

Table of Contents

Chapter 1
Ways to Receive God's Answers · 1

Chapter 2
We Still Need to Ask Him · 13

Chapter 3
The Spiritual Law on God's Answers · 23

Chapter 4
Destroy the Wall of Sin · 37

Chapter 5

You Reap What You Have Sowed · 49

Chapter 6

Elijah Receives God's Answer by Fire · 63

Chapter 7

How to Fulfill the Desires of Your Heart · 73

Chapter 1

Ways to Receive God's Answers

1 John 3:18-22

"Little children, let us not love with word or with tongue, but in deed and truth. We will know by this that we are of the truth, and will assure our heart before Him in whatever our heart condemns us; for God is greater than our heart and knows all things. Beloved, if our heart does not condemn us, we have confidence before God; and whatever we ask we receive from Him, because we keep His commandments and do the things that are pleasing in His sight."

One of the sources of great joy for God's children is the fact that the almighty God is alive, answers their prayer, and in all things works for their good. People who believe in this fact pray zealously so that they may receive anything for which they ask from God and give glory to Him to their hearts' content.

1 John 5:14 tells us, *"This is the confidence which we have before Him, that, if we ask anything according to His will, He hears us."* The verse reminds us that when we ask according to God's will, we have the right to receive anything from Him. No matter how evil a parent may be, when her son asks for bread she will not give him a stone, and when he asks for fish the mother will not give him a snake. What, then, could possibly prevent God from giving His children good gifts when they ask Him for them?

When the Canaanite woman in Matthew 15:21-28 came before Jesus, she not only received answers to her prayer but also fulfilled the desires of her heart. Even though her daughter was suffering from terrible demon-possession, the woman asked Jesus to heal her daughter because she believed everything was possible for those who believed. What do you suppose Jesus did for this Gentile woman who asked Him for her daughter's healing without giving up? As we find in John 16:23, *"In that day you will not question Me about anything. Truly, truly, I say to you, if you ask the Father for anything in My name, He will give it to you,"* upon seeing the woman's faith Jesus immediately granted her request. *"O woman, your faith is great; it shall be done for you as you wish"* (Matthew 15:28).

How marvelous and sweet God's answer is!

If we believe in the living God, as His children we must give glory to Him by receiving everything for which we ask Him. With the passage on which this chapter is based, let us explore the ways in which we can receive God's answers.

We Must Believe in God Who Promises to Answer Us

Through the Bible, God promised us that He would certainly answer our prayer and pleas. Therefore, only when we do not doubt this promise can we zealously ask and receive everything for which we ask from God.

Numbers 23:19 reads, *"God is not a man, that He should lie, nor a son of man, that He should repent; Has He said, and will He not do it? Or has He spoken, and will He not make it good?"* In Matthew 7:7-8 God promises us, *"Ask, and it will be given to you; seek, and you will find; knock, and it will be opened to you. For everyone who asks receives, and he who seeks finds, and to him who knocks it will be opened."*

Throughout the Bible are many references pointing to God's promise, that He would answer us if we ask according to His will. The following are a few examples:

Therefore I say to you, all things for which you pray and

ask, believe that you have received them, and they will be granted you (Mark 11:24).

If you abide in Me, and My words abide in you, ask whatever you wish, and it will be done for you (John 15:7).

Whatever you ask in My name, that will I do, so that the Father may be glorified in the Son (John 14:13).

Then you will call upon Me and come and pray to Me, and I will listen to you. You will seek Me and find Me when you search for Me with all your heart (Jeremiah 29:12-13).

Call upon Me in the day of trouble; I shall rescue you, and you will honor Me (Psalm 50:15).

God's such promise is found time and again in both Old and New Testaments. Even if there were only one biblical verse regarding this promise, we would hold fast to that verse and pray to receive His answers. However, for this promise is found numerous times throughout the Bible, we must believe that God is indeed alive and that He works the same yesterday and today and forever (Hebrews 13:8).

Moreover, the Bible tells us of many blessed men and women who believed in God's Word, asked, and received His answers.

We ought to take after the faith and the heart of these people and lead our own lives in which we always receive His answers.

When Jesus told a paralytic in Mark 2:1-12, *"Your sins are forgiven. Get up, pick up your pallet and go home,"* the paralytic got up, took his pallet and walked out in full view of them all, and all the witnesses were amazed and could only praise God.

A centurion in Matthew 8:5-13 came before Jesus for his servant who was lying paralyzed at home, fearfully tormented and told Him, *"Just say the word, and my servant will be healed"* (v. 8). We know that when Jesus said to the centurion, *"Go! It shall be done for you as you have believed,"* the centurion's servant was healed at that very hour (v. 13).

A leper in Mark 1:40-42 came to Jesus and begged Him on his knees, *"If You are willing, You can make me clean"* (v. 40). As He became filled with compassion for the leper, Jesus reached out His hand and touched the man, *"I am willing; be cleansed!"* (v. 41). We find that the leprosy left the man and he was cured.

God allows all people to receive whatever they ask Him in the name of Jesus Christ. God also wishes all people to believe in Him who has promised to answer their prayer, pray with an unchanging heart without giving up, and become His blessed children.

Types of Prayer to Which God Does Not Answer

When people believe and pray according to God's will, live by His Word, and die just as a kernel of wheat dies, God takes notice of their heart and dedication and answers their prayer. Yet, if there are individuals who cannot receive God's answers despite their prayer, what could be the cause? There were many people in the Bible who failed to receive His answers even though they prayed. By examining the reasons for which people fail to receive God's answers, we must learn how we can receive answers from Him.

First, if we harbor sin in our heart and pray, God tells us He will not answer our prayer. Psalm 66:18 tells us, *"If I regard wickedness in my heart, the LORD will not hear,"* and Isaiah 59:1-2 reminds us, *"Behold, the LORD's hand is not so short That it cannot save; nor is His ear so dull that it cannot hear. But your iniquities have made a separation between you and your God, and your sins have hidden His face from you so that He does not hear."* For the enemy devil will intercept our prayer because of our sin, it only beats the air and will not reach God's throne.

Second, if we pray amidst a discord with our brothers, God will not answer us. For our heavenly Father will not forgive us unless we forgive our brothers from our heart (Matthew 18:35), our prayer can neither be delivered to God nor be answered.

Third, if we pray to satisfy our cravings, God does not answer our prayer. If we disregard His glory but instead pray in accordance with the desires of the sinful nature and to spend what we receive from Him for our pleasure, God will not answer us (James 4:2-3). For instance, to an obedient and studious daughter the father will give an allowance whenever she asks for it. To a disobedient daughter who does not care much for studying, however, the father will be either unwilling to give her an allowance or worried sick that she might spend the allowance with wrong motives. By the same token, if we ask for anything with wrong motives and to satisfy the desires of the sinful nature, God does not answer us because we may go down the path that leads to destruction.

Fourth, we should neither pray nor cry out for idolaters (Jeremiah 11:10-11). For God detests idols above all else, we only need to pray for the salvation of their souls. Any other prayer or requests made for them or on their behalf will go unanswered.

Fifth, God does not answer prayer that is filled with doubts because we can receive answers from the Lord only when we believe and do not doubt (James 1:6-7). I am sure many of you have borne witness to the healing of incurable diseases and the resolution of seemingly impossible problems when people asked God to intervene. This is because God told us that *"Truly I say to you, whoever says to this mountain, 'Be taken up and cast into the sea,' and does not doubt in his heart, but believes that what he says is going to happen, it will be granted him"* (Mark 11:23). You ought to know that prayer filled with doubts cannot be answered and that only the prayer in accordance with God's will brings an undeniable sense of certainty.

Sixth, if we do not obey God's commands, our prayer will not be answered. When we obey God's commands and do what pleases Him, the Bible tells us that we can have confidence before God and receive from Him anything we ask (1 John 3:21-22). For Proverbs 8:17 tells us, *"I love those who love me; and those who diligently seek me will find me,"* prayer of people who obey God's commands in their love for Him (1 John 5:3) will surely be answered.

Seventh, we cannot receive God's answers without sowing. For Galatians 6:7 reads, *"Do not be deceived, God is not mocked; for whatever a man sows, this he will also reap,"* and 2 Corinthians 9:6 tells us, *"Now this I say, he who sows sparingly will also reap sparingly, and he who sows bountifully will also reap bountifully,"* without sowing one cannot reap. If one sows prayer, his soul will get along well; if he sows offerings, he will receive financial blessings; and if he sows with his deed, he will receive blessings of good health. In sum, you must sow what you wish to reap and sow accordingly to receive God's answers.

In addition to the conditions above, if people fail to pray in the name of Jesus Christ or fail to pray from their heart, or keep on babbling, their prayer will not be answered. A discord between a husband and a wife (1 Peter 3:7) or disobedience does not warrant them God's answers.

We must always keep in mind that such conditions above create a wall between God and us; He will turn His face away from us and not answer our prayer. Therefore, we must first seek God's kingdom and righteousness, call out to Him in prayer to achieve the desires of our heart, and always receive His answers by holding fast to the end in firm faith.

Secrets to Receiving Answers to Our Prayer

At the beginning phase of one's life in Christ, spiritually he is comparable to an infant, and God answers his prayer right away. For the person does not yet know the whole truth, if he puts into action the Word of God he learns even a little, God answers him as if he were an infant crying for milk, and leads him to meet God. As he continuously hears and understands the truth, he will grow out of the "toddler" phase, and as much as he puts the truth into action, God will answer him. If an individual has grown out of a "child" stage spiritually but keeps sinning and fails to live by the Word, he cannot receive God's answers; from that point on, he will see God's answers as much as he accomplishes sanctification.

Therefore, in order for people who have not received answers to receive His answers, they must first repent, turn from their ways, and begin leading obedient lives in which they live by God's Word. When they dwell in the truth after repenting by rending of their heart, God gives amazing blessings to them. For Job only had faith that was stored as knowledge, at first he grumbled against God when trials and suffering came his way. After Job met God and repented by rending his heart, he forgave his friends and lived by God's Word. In turn, God blessed Job twice as much as he had had before (Job 42:5-10).

Jonah found himself confined in a great fish because of his disobedience to God's Word. Yet, when he prayed, repented, and gave thanks in his prayer by faith, God commanded the fish, and it vomited Jonah onto dry land (Jonah 2:1-10).

When we turn from our ways, repent, live by the Father's will, believe, and call out to Him, the enemy devil will come at you from one direction but flee from you in seven. Naturally, diseases, problems with our children, and problems with finance will be resolved. A persecuting husband turns into a good and warm husband and a peaceful family emanating Christ's aroma will give great glory to God.

If we have turned from our ways, repented, and received His answers to our prayer, we must give glory to God by testifying to our joy. When we please and give glory to Him through our testimony, God not only receives the glory and delights in us but He also becomes eager to ask us, "What shall I give you?"

Suppose a parent gave her son a gift and the son did not appear grateful or express his gratitude in any way. The mother may not want to give him anything else. However, if the son became very appreciative of the gift and pleased his mother, she becomes all the more delighted and wishes to give her son more gifts and prepares accordingly. By the same token, we will receive all the more from Him when we give glory to Him remembering that our Father God delights in His children's receiving answers to their prayer and gives even more good gifts to those who testify to His answers.

Let all of us ask according to God's will, show Him our faith and dedication, and receive from Him whatever we ask. Showing God our faith and dedication may seem a difficult task from man's perspective. However, only after such a process as we throw away heavy sins that stand against the truth, fix our eyes on the everlasting Heaven, receive answers to our prayer, and build our rewards in the heavenly kingdom, will our lives be filled with gratitude and joy and truly worthwhile. Moreover, our lives will be all the more blessed because trials and sufferings will have been driven away and true comfort can be felt in God's guidance and protection.

May each of you ask by faith whatever you desire, pray earnestly, fight sin and obey God's commands in order to receive everything you ask, please Him in every affair, and give great glory to Him, in the name of Jesus Christ I pray!

Chapter 2

We Still Need to Ask Him

Ezekiel 36:31-37

Then you will remember your evil ways and your deeds that were not good, and you will loathe yourselves in your own sight for your iniquities and your abominations. "I am not doing this for your sake," declares the LORD God, "let it be known to you. Be ashamed and confounded for your ways, O house of Israel!" Thus says the LORD God, "On the day that I cleanse you from all your iniquities, I will cause the cities to be inhabited, and the waste places will be rebuilt. The desolate land will be cultivated instead of being a desolation in the sight of everyone who passes by. They will say, 'This desolate land has become like the garden of Eden; and the waste, desolate and ruined cities are fortified and inhabited.' Then the nations that are left round about you will know that I, the LORD, have rebuilt the ruined places and planted that which was desolate; I, the LORD, have spoken and will do it." Thus says the LORD God, "This also I will let the house of Israel ask Me to do for them: I will increase their men like a flock."

Through the sixty-six books of the Bible, God who is the same yesterday, today, and forever (Hebrews 13:8) testifies to the fact that He is alive and at work. To all those who have believed in His Word and obeyed it in Old Testament times, in New Testament times, and today, God has faithfully shown them the evidence of His work.

God the Creator of everything in the universe and Governor of life, death, curse, and blessing of mankind has promised to "bless" us (Deuteronomy 28:5-6) as long as we believe in and obey all of His Word found in the Bible. Now, if we truly believed in this amazing and wonderful fact, what could we lack and what could we not receive? We find in Numbers 23:19, *"God is not a man, that He should lie, nor a son of man, that He should repent; Has He said, and will He not do it? Or has He spoken, and will He not make it good?"* Does God speak and not act? Does He promise and not fulfill? Furthermore, since Jesus promised us in John 16:23, *"Truly, truly, I say to you, if you ask the Father for anything in My name, He will give it to you,"* God's children are truly blessed.

Thus, it is only natural for the children of God to lead lives in which they receive whatever they ask and give glory to their heavenly Father. Why, then, do most Christians fail to lead such lives? With the passage on which this chapter is based, let us explore how we can always receive God's answers.

God Has Spoken and Will Do It but We Still Need to Ask Him

As God's elect, the people of Israel have received abundant blessings. They were promised that if they fully obeyed and followed God's Word, He would set them high above all the nations on earth, grant the enemies who rise up against them to be defeated before them, and bless everything they put their hand to (Deuteronomy 28:1, 7, 8). Such blessings came upon the Israelites when they obeyed God's Word, but when they did wrong, disobeyed the Law, and worshipped idols, in God's anger they were taken captive and their land was ruined.

At that time, God told the Israelites that if they repented and turned from their wicked ways, He would allow the desolate land to be cultivated and ruined places to be rebuilt. Moreover, God said *"I, the LORD, have spoken and will do it. ... This also I will let the house of Israel ask Me to do for them"* (Ezekiel 36:36-37).

Why did God promise the Israelites He would act but also say that they would still have to "ask" Him?

Even though God knows what we need before we even ask Him (Matthew 6:8), He has also told us, *"Ask, and it will be given to you; seek, and you will find; knock, and it will be opened to you. For everyone who asks receives, and he who seeks finds, and to him who knocks it will be opened. Or what man is there among you who, when his son asks for a loaf, will give him a stone? Or if he asks for a fish, he will not give him a snake, will he? If you then, being evil, know how to give good gifts to your children, how much more will your Father who is in heaven give what is good to those who ask Him!"* (Matthew 7:7-11)

In addition, as God has told us throughout the Bible we would need to ask and call out to Him in order to receive His answers (Jeremiah 33:3; John 14:14), God's children who truly believe in His Word must still ask God even though He has spoken and said He would act.

On the one hand, when God says "I will do it," if we believe and obey His Word, we will receive the answers. On the other hand, if we doubt, test God, and fail to be grateful and instead complain in times of trial and suffering – in sum, if we fail to believe in God's promise – we cannot receive God's answers. Even if God has promised "I will do it," that promise can be fulfilled only when we hold fast to that pledge in prayer and in deed. One cannot be said to have faith if he does not ask but merely looks to that promise and says, "Since God said so, it will be done." Nor can he receive God's answers because there is no deed accompanied.

We Must Ask to Receive God's Answers

First, you must pray to destroy the wall that stands between you and God.

When Daniel was taken captive in Babylon after the fall of Jerusalem, he came across the Scriptures containing the prophecy of Jeremiah and learned that the desolation of Jerusalem would last seventy years. During those seventy years, as Daniel learned, Israel would serve the king of Babylon. When the seventy years were up, however, the king of Babylon, his kingdom, and the land of the Chaldeans would become cursed and perpetually desolate because of their sins. Even though the Israelites were held captive in Babylon at the time, Jeremiah's prophecy that they would become independent and return to their homeland after seventy years was an instant source of joy and relief for Daniel.

Yet, Daniel did not, although he could easily have, share his joy with his fellow Israelites. Instead, Daniel vowed to plead with God by prayer and supplications, with fasting, sackcloth and ashes. And he repented for his and the Israelites' having sinned, done wrong, been wicked, rebelled, and turned away from God's commands and laws (Daniel 9:3-19).

God had revealed through Prophet Jeremiah not how Israel's captivity in Babylon would end; He had only prophesied the end of captivity after seven decades. For Daniel knew the law of the spiritual realm, however, he was well aware that the wall that stood between Israel and God had first to be destroyed in order for God's Word to be fulfilled. By doing so, Daniel showed his faith by deed. As Daniel fasted and repented – for himself and the rest of the Israelites – for having done wrong against God and been subsequently cursed, God destroyed that wall, answered

Daniel, gave the Israelites "seventy 'sevens' [weeks]," and revealed other secrets to him.

As we become God's children who ask according to our Father's Word, we ought to realize that destroying the wall of sin precedes receiving any answers to our prayer and make destroying that wall a priority.

Second, we must pray by faith and in obedience.

In Exodus 3:6-8 we read of God's promise to the people of Israel, who at the time were enslaved in Egypt, that He would bring them out of Egypt and lead them to Canaan, the land flowing with milk and honey. Canaan is a land God promised the Israelites to give them as a possession (Exodus 6:8). He promised on oath to give the land to their descendants and commanded them to go up (Exodus 33:1-3). It is a promised land where God commanded Israel to destroy all idols therein and warned them against making a covenant with people already living there and their gods, so that the Israelites would not create a snare between themselves and their God. This was a promise from God who always fulfills what He promises. Why, then, were the Israelites unable to enter Canaan?

In their unbelief in God and His power, the people of Israel grumbled against Him (Numbers 14:1-3) and disobeyed Him, and thus failed to enter Canaan while standing on its threshold (Numbers 14:21-23; Hebrews 3:18-19). In short, even though God had promised the Israelites the land of Canaan, that promise was of no use if they did not believe or obey Him. If they did believe and obey Him, that promise would have surely been fulfilled. In the end, only Joshua and Caleb who believed in God's Word, along with the descendants of the Israelites, could enter Canaan (Joshua 14:6-12). Through Israel's history, let us keep in mind that we can receive God's answers only when we ask Him by trusting His promise and in obedience, and receive His answers by asking Him by faith.

Although Moses himself surely believed in God's promise on Canaan, because the Israelites did not believe in God's power, even he was prohibited from entering the promised land. God's work is at times answered by the faith of one man but at other times answered only when everyone involved possesses faith that suffices the manifestation of His work. In entering Canaan, God required the faith of the entire Israelites, not just that of Moses. Yet, for He could not find this kind of faith among the people of Israel, God did not allow their entrance to Canaan. Keep in mind that when God seeks the faith of not just one individual but that of everyone involved, all people need to pray by faith and in obedience, and become one in heart in order to receive His answers.

When a woman who had been suffering from 12 years of bleeding received healing by touching Jesus' cloak, He asked, *"Who touched My garments?"* and had her testify to her healing in front of all the people gathered (Mark 5:25-34).

An individual's testifying to God's work manifested in his life helps others grow their own faith and strengthens them to transform themselves into people of prayer who ask and receive His answers. For receiving God's answers by faith enables unbelievers to possess faith and meet the living God, it is a truly magnificent way to give glory to Him.

By believing in and obeying the Word of blessing found in the Bible, and keeping in mind that we still need to ask even though God has promised us, "I have spoken and I will do it," let us always receive His answers, become His blessed children, and give glory to Him to our hearts' content.

Chapter 3

The Spiritual Law on God's Answers

Luke 22:39-46

And [Jesus] came out and proceeded as was His custom to the Mount of Olives; and the disciples also followed Him. When He arrived at the place, He said to them, "Pray that you may not enter into temptation." And He withdrew from them about a stone's throw, and He knelt down and began to pray, saying, "Father, if You are willing, remove this cup from Me; yet not My will, but Yours be done." Now an angel from heaven appeared to Him, strengthening Him. And being in agony He was praying very fervently; and His sweat became like drops of blood, falling down upon the ground. When He rose from prayer, He came to the disciples and found them sleeping from sorrow, and said to them, "Why are you sleeping? Get up and pray that you may not enter into temptation."

God's children receive salvation and have the right to receive from God whatever they ask by faith. That is why we read in Matthew 21:22, *"And all things you ask in prayer, believing, you will receive."*

Yet, many people wonder why they do not receive God's answers after praying, question whether their prayer has been delivered to God, or doubt whether God has even heard their prayer.

Just as we need to know proper methods and routes to go on a trouble-free journey to a certain destination, only when we become aware of proper methods and routes of prayer can we receive His prompt answers. Prayer itself does not guarantee God's answers; we need to learn the law of the spiritual realm on His answers and pray in accordance with that law.

Let us explore the law of the spiritual realm on God's answers and its relationship with the seven Spirits of God.

The Law of the Spiritual Realm on God's Answers

For prayer is asking the almighty God for things we desire and need, we can receive His answers only when we ask Him in accordance with the law of the spiritual realm. No amount or degree of man's effort based on his thoughts, methods, fame, and knowledge will ever bring him God's answers.

Because God is a righteous Judge (Psalm 7:11), hears our prayer, and answers it, He requires of us a befitting sum in exchange for His answers. God's answers to our prayer can be compared to purchasing meat from a butcher. If the butcher is likened to God, the scale he uses can be a device with which God measures, based on the law of the spiritual realm, whether or not one can receive His answers.

Suppose we went to a butcher to purchase two pounds of beef. When we ask him for the amount of meat we require, the butcher weighs the meat and sees whether or not the meat he has gathered weighs two pounds. If the meat on the scale does weigh two pounds, the butcher receives from us the appropriate sum of money for the two pounds of beef, wraps the meat, and gives it to us.

By the same token, while God does answer our prayer, He without fail receives something from us in return that warrants His answers. This is the law of the spiritual realm on God's answers.

God hears our prayer, accepts from us something of a befitting value, and then answers us. If one has yet to receive God's answers to his prayer, this is because he has not yet presented God a sum befitting His answers. Since the amount necessary in receiving His answers varies depending on the content of one's prayer, until he receives the kind of faith by which he can receive God's answers, he must pray on and accumulate that necessary sum. Even though we do not know in detail the befitting sum of which God requires us, He does. Therefore, as we pay closest attention to the voice of the Holy Spirit, we need to ask God for some things with fasting, certain things with vowed nightly prayer, others with prayer of tears, and still others with thanksgiving offerings. Such deed accumulates the sum required to receive God's answers, as He gives us the kind of faith by which we can believe and blesses us with His answers.

Even if two people set aside and begin a time of vowed prayer, one receives God's answers immediately after he begins vowed prayer, while another fails to receive His answers even after her time of vowed prayer has come and gone. What explanations can we find for this disparity?

For God is wise and makes His plans in advance, if God declares that an individual possesses a heart that will keep praying until the period of vowed prayer is up, He will answer the person's request right away. Yet, if one fails to receive God's answers for a problem she faces now, that is because she has failed to wholly give God a befitting sum for His answers. When we vow to pray for a certain period of time, we ought to know God has led our hearts so that He would receive the befitting sum of prayer for His answers. Consequently, if we fail to accumulate that sum, we fail to receive God's answers.

For instance, if a man prays for his future spouse, God seeks for him a proper bride and prepares so that He may work for the man's good in all things. This does not mean that the proper bride appears before the man's eyes even though he is not yet of the age to get married only because he has prayed for her. For God answers those who believe they have received His answers, at the time of His choosing He will reveal His work to them.

However, when one's prayer is not in line with His will, no amount of prayer will warrant God's answers. If that same man sought and prayed for his future bride's such outward conditions as educational background, appearance, wealth, fame, and the like – in other words, prayer filled with greed formed within the frame of his mind – God will not answer him.

Even if two people prayed to God with the same exact problem, for the degree of their sanctification and the measure of faith by which they can wholly believe are different, the amount of prayer God receives is also different (Revelation 5:8). One may receive God's answers in a month's time while the other would in a day's time.

Furthermore, the greater the significance of God's answers to one's prayer, the greater the amount of his prayer must be. According to the law of the spiritual realm, a great vessel will be tested greater and come forth as gold while a small vessel will be tested on a smaller scale and just a little used by God. Therefore, no one must judge others and say, "Look at all his hardships despite his faithfulness!" and disappoint God in any way. Among our forefathers of faith, Moses was tested for 40 years and Jacob for 20 years, and we know how suitable a vessel each became in God's sight and was used for His great purpose after enduring their respective trials. Think of the process in which a national soccer team is formed and trained. If skills of a particular player is worthy of putting him on the roster, only after more time and effort invested in training will he be able to represent his country.

Whether the answer we seek from God is big or small, we must move His heart to receive His answers. In praying to receive whatever we ask for, God will be moved and answer us when we give Him befitting sums of prayer, cleanse our hearts to have no wall of sin standing between God and us, and give Him thanksgiving, joy, offerings, and the like as a token of our faith in Him.

The Relationship between the Law of the Spiritual Realm and the Seven Spirits

As we have examined with the metaphor of the butcher and his scale above, according to the law of the spiritual realm God measures the amount of everyone's prayer without an error and determines whether the person has accumulated a befitting sum of prayer. While most people make judgments on a particular object only by what is visible to their eyes, God makes an accurate assessment with the seven Spirits of God (Revelation 5:6). In other words, when one is declared qualified by the seven Spirits, he is given God's answers to his prayer.

What do the seven Spirits measure?

First, the seven Spirits measure one's faith.

In faith, there are 'spiritual faith' and 'fleshly faith.' The kind of faith the seven Spirits measure is not faith as knowledge –

fleshly faith – but spiritual faith that is alive and accompanied by works (James 2:22). For example, there is a scene in Mark 9 in which the father of a child who was possessed with demons which had made him mute came before Jesus (Mark 9:17). The father said to Jesus, "I do believe; help my unbelief!" Here the father confessed his fleshly faith, saying, "I do believe" and asked Him for spiritual faith, saying, "Help my unbelief!" Jesus answered the father right away and healed the boy (Mark 9:18-27).

It is impossible to please God without faith (Hebrews 11:6). Yet, for we can fulfill the desires of our hearts when we do please Him, by the faith that can please God we can achieve the desires of our hearts. Therefore, if we do not receive God's answers even though He has told us, *"It shall be done for you as you have believed,"* it means our faith has not yet been made complete (Matthew 8:13).

Second, the seven Spirits measure one's joy.

For 1 Thessalonians 5:16 tells us to rejoice always, it is God's will for us to rejoice always. Instead of being joyful in difficult times, many Christians today find themselves confined in anxiety, fear, and worry. If they truly believe in the living God with all their heart, they can always be joyous regardless of the situation in which they find themselves. They can be joyous in a fervent hope that lies in the everlasting heavenly kingdom, not in this world that is to pass away in a short while.

Third, the seven Spirits measure one's prayer.

For God tells us to pray without ceasing (1 Thessalonians 5:17) and promises to give to those who ask Him (Matthew 7:7), it only makes sense to receive from God what we ask for in prayer. The kind of prayer with which God is pleased entails praying habitually (Luke 22:39) and kneeling down to pray in line with God's will. With such an attitude and posture, we will naturally call out to God with all our heart and our prayer will be of faith and love. God examines this kind of prayer. We are not to pray only when we want something or are saddened and babble in prayer, but pray according to God's will (Luke 22:39-41).

Fourth, the seven Spirits measure one's thanksgiving.

For God has commanded us to give thanks in everything (1 Thessalonians 5:18), anyone with faith ought to naturally give thanks in everything with all his heart. Since He has moved us from the path to destruction onto the path to eternal life, how could we not be grateful? We are to be grateful for God's meeting with those who earnestly seek Him and His answering to those who ask Him. Moreover, even if we face difficulties during our brief life in this world, we are to be grateful because our hope is in the everlasting Heaven.

Fifth, the seven Spirits measure whether or not one keeps God's commands.

1 John 5:2 tells us, *"By this we know that we love the*

children of God, when we love God and observe His commandments," and God's commandments are not burdensome if we love Him (1 John 5:3). One's habitual prayer on his knees and calling out to God is prayer of love derived from his faith. By his faith and in his love for God, he will pray in accordance with His Word.

Yet, many people complain about the lack of God's answers when they are heading west even though the Bible tells them, "Go east." All they need to do is to believe what the Bible tells them and obey it. For they are quick to put God's Word aside, assess each situation according to their own thoughts and theories, and pray according to their own benefits, God turns His face away from them and does not answer them. Suppose you promised to meet your friend at a train station in New York City but subsequently realized you prefer the bus to the train, and took the bus to New York instead. No matter how long you wait at the bus station, you will never be able to meet your friend. If you went west even after God had told you, "Go east," you cannot be said to have obeyed Him. Yet, it is tragic and heartbreaking to see so many Christians possess such faith. This is neither faith nor love. If we say we love God, it is only natural for us to keep His commands (John 14:15; 1 John 5:3).

Love for God will drive you to pray all the more zealously and diligently. This in turn will bear fruit in the salvation of souls and evangelization, and the accomplishment of God's kingdom and righteousness. And your soul will prosper and you will receive the power of prayer. Because you receive the answer and give glory to God and because you believe all this will be rewarded in Heaven, you will be grateful and not grow weary. Thus, if we profess our belief in God, it is only natural for us to obey the Ten Commandments, the précis of the sixty-six books of the Bible.

Sixth, the seven Spirits measure one's faithfulness.

God wants us to be faithful not just in a particular area but be faithful in all His house. Furthermore, as recorded in 1 Corinthians 4:2, *"In this case, moreover, it is required of stewards that one be found trustworthy,"* it is proper for those with God-given duties to ask God to strengthen them to be found faithful in everything and trustworthy by the people around them. In addition, they should ask for faithfulness at home and work and, as they strive to be faithful in everything in which they play a part, their faithfulness must be accomplished in the truth.

Seventh and last, the seven Spirits measure one's love.

Even if one is qualified according to the six standards above, God tells us that without love we are "nothing" but "a clanging cymbal," and that the greatest among faith, hope, and love is love. Moreover, Jesus fulfilled the law in love (Romans 13:10) and as His children it is only right for us to love each other.

In order to receive God's answers to our prayer, we must first be qualified when measured against the standards of the seven Spirits. Does this mean that new believers, who do not yet know the truth, are unable to receive God's answers?

Suppose a toddler who cannot speak, one day pronounce very clearly, "Mommy!" His parents would be so delighted and give their child anything he desires.

By the same token, since there are different levels of faith, the seven Spirits measure each one and answer accordingly. Therefore, God is moved and delighted to answer a novice when she displays even small faith. God is moved and delighted to answer when believers at the second or third level of faith have accumulated their corresponding measure of faith. Believers at the fourth or fifth level of faith, as they live by God's will and pray in an even more befitting way to Him, are instantly qualified in the sight of the seven Spirits and receive God's answers more quickly.

In sum, the higher level of faith at which one finds himself – as he is that much more aware of the law of the spiritual realm and lives by it – the more quickly he receives God's answers. Yet, for what reasons do novices often receive God's answers more quickly? By the grace he receives from God, a new believer becomes filled with the Holy Spirit and qualified in sight of the seven Spirits and thus receives God's answers more quickly.

However, as he goes deeper into the truth he becomes slothful and gradually loses the first love as the zeal he once had grows cold and a tendency of "making up as you go along" develops.

In our ardor for God, let us become proper in the sight of the seven Spirits by zealously living by the truth, receive from our Father everything we ask for in prayer, and lead blessed lives in which we give glory to Him!

Chapter 4

Destroy the Wall of Sin

Isaiah 59:1-2

*"Behold, the LORD's hand is not so short
That it cannot save;
Nor is His ear so dull That it cannot hear.
But your iniquities have made a separation
between you and your God,
And your sins have hidden His face from you
so that He does not hear."*

God tells His children in Matthew 7:7-8, *"Ask, and it will be given to you; seek, and you will find; knock, and it will be opened to you. For everyone who asks receives, and he who seeks finds, and to him who knocks it will be opened"* and promises them to answer their prayer. Yet, why do many people fail to receive God's answers to their prayer despite His promise?

God does not hear the prayer of sinners; He turns His face away from them. He is also unable to answer the prayer of people who have a wall of sin standing in their path to God. Therefore, in order to enjoy good health and that all may go well with us even as our souls prosper, destroying the wall of sin blocking our way to God must be a priority.

By exploring various elements that have taken part in constructing the wall of sin, I urge each of you to become God's blessed child who repents of his sins if there is a wall of sin between God and himself, receives everything he asks God in prayer, and gives glory to Him.

Destroy the Wall of Sin for Your Unbelief in God and Not Accepting the Lord as Your Savior

The Bible dictates that it is a sin for anyone not to believe in God and accept Jesus Christ as his Savior (John 16:9). Many people say, "I am sinless because I've led a good life," but in spiritual ignorance they make such remarks without knowing the nature of sin. For the Word of God is not in their heart, these individuals do not know the difference between true right and true wrong and cannot distinguish good from evil. Furthermore, without knowing true righteousness, if the standards of this world tell them, "You are not that evil," they can say without reservation that they are good. No matter how good a life one may believe he has led, when he looks back at his life under the light of God's Word after accepting Jesus Christ, he discovers that his life has not been "good" at all. This is because he realizes that his not having believed in God and accepted Jesus Christ is the greatest of all sins. God is obligated to answer the prayer of people who have accepted Jesus Christ and become His children, while the children of God have the right to receive His answers to their prayer according to His promise.

The reason God's children – who believe in Him and have accepted Jesus Christ as their Savior – are unable to receive answers to their prayer is because they fail to recognize the existence of a wall, which has stemmed from their sin and evil, standing between God and themselves. That is why even when they fast or stay up all night in prayer, God turns His face away from them and does not answer their prayer.

Destroy the Sin of Failing to Love One Another

God tells us that it is only natural for His children to love one another (1 John 4:11). In addition, because He tells us to love even our enemies (Mathew 5:44), hating our brothers instead of loving them is disobeying God's Word and thus constitutes a sin. For Jesus Christ showed His love through the crucifixion for mankind, who was confined in sin and evil, it is right for us to love our parents, brothers, and children. Yet, it is a grave sin before God to harbor such frivolous emotions as hatred and unwillingness to forgive each other. God has not commanded us to show Him the kind of love by which Jesus died on the cross to redeem man from his sins; He has merely asked us to turn hatred into forgiveness of others. Why, then, is this so difficult?

God tells us that anyone who hates his brothers is a "murderer" (1 John 3:15), and that in the same way our Father will treat us unless we forgive our brothers (Matthew 18:35), and urges us to harbor love and stay away from grumbling against our brothers to avoid judgment (James 5:9).

For the Holy Spirit dwells in each of us, by the love of Jesus who was crucified and has redeemed us from our sins of the past, the present, and the future, we can love all people when we repent before Him, turn from our ways, and receive His forgiveness. For the people of this world do not believe in Jesus Christ, however, there is no forgiveness for them even if they should repent, and they are unable to share true love with one another without the guidance of the Holy Spirit.

Even if your brother hates you, you have to possess the kind of heart by which you stand by the truth, understand and forgive him, and pray for him in love, so that you do not become a sinner yourself. If we hate our brothers instead of loving them, we will have sinned before God, lose the fullness of the Holy Spirit, become wretched and foolish spending all of our days lamenting. Neither should we expect God to answer our prayer.

Only by the aid of the Holy Spirit can we come to love, understand, and forgive our brothers and receive from God whatever we ask in prayer.

Destroying the Wall of Sin of Disobeying God's Commands

In John 14:21, Jesus tells us, *"He who has My commandments and keeps them is the one who loves Me; and he who loves Me will be loved by My Father, and I will love him and will disclose Myself to him."* For this reason, 1 John 3:21 tells us that *"Beloved, if our heart does not condemn us, we have confidence before God."* In other words, if a wall of sin has been created because of our disobedience to God's commands, we cannot receive His answers to our prayer. Only when God's children obey their Father's commands and do what is pleasing to Him can they ask Him for anything they desire with confidence and receive whatever they ask.

1 John 3:24 reminds us, *"The one who keeps His commandments abides in Him, and He in him. We know by this that He abides in us, by the Spirit whom He has given us."* It stresses that only when one's heart is filled with the truth by wholly giving our Lord his heart and he lives by the guidance of

the Holy Spirit, can he receive everything for which he asks and his life be successful in every way.

For instance, if there were a hundred rooms in one's heart and he gave all hundred of them to the Lord, his soul would prosper and he receive the blessing of everything's going well for him. Yet, if the same person gave the Lord fifty of the rooms in his heart and used the other fifty at his disposal, he could not always receive God's answers because he will only receive the Holy Spirit's guidance half the time while he uses the other fifty to ask God in his thought or in accordance with the lustful desires of the flesh. For our Lord dwells in each of us, even if there is an obstacle before us He strengthens us to either go around or run over it. Even if we go through the valley of the shadow He gives us a way to avoid it, works for our good in all things, and leads our ways to prosper.

When we please God by obeying His commands, we live in God and He lives in us, and we can give glory to Him as we receive everything we ask for in prayer. Let us destroy the wall of sin of disobeying God's commands, begin obeying them, become confident before God, and give glory to Him by receiving everything we ask.

Destroy the Wall of Sin of Praying to Satisfy Your Cravings

God tells us to do everything in life for His glory (1

Corinthians 10:31). If we pray for anything except for His glory, we are seeking to fulfill our cravings and desires of the flesh, and cannot receive God's answers to such requests (James 4:3).

On the one hand, if you seek material blessings for God's kingdom and His righteousness, the relief to the poor, and the salvation effort of souls, you will receive God's answers because you are in fact seeking His glory. On the other hand, if you seek material blessings in hopes of boasting to a brother who rebukes you, "How can you be poor when you go to church?" you are in fact praying in accordance with evil to satisfy your cravings, and there will be no answers to your prayer. Even in this world, parents who truly love their child will not give him $100 to squander at an arcade. By the same token, God does not want His children to walk down the wrong path and for this reason He does not answer every request His children make.

1 John 5:14-15 tells us, *"This is the confidence which we have before Him, that, if we ask anything according to His will, He hears us. And if we know that He hears us in whatever we ask, we know that we have the requests which we have asked from Him."* Only when we discard our cravings and pray according to God's will and for His glory, will we receive anything we ask Him in prayer.

Destroy the Wall of Sin of Doubting in Prayer

For God is pleased when we show Him our faith, without

faith it is impossible to please God (Hebrews 11:6). Even from the Bible we can find many instances in which God's answers found their way to people who showed Him their faith (Matthew 20:29-34; Mark 5:22-43, 9:17-27, 10:46-52). When people failed to show their faith in God, they were rebuked for their "little faith" even if they were Jesus' disciples (Matthew 8:23-27). When people showed God their great faith in Him, even the Gentile was commended (Matthew 15:28).

God rebukes those who are unable to believe but rather doubt even a little (Mark 9:16-29), and tells us that if we harbor even an ounce of doubt while praying, we should not think we will receive anything from the Lord (James 1:6-7). In other words, even if we fast and pray through the night, if our prayer is filled with doubts, we should not even expect to receive God's answers.

Moreover, God reminds us, *"I tell you the truth, if anyone says to this mountain, 'Go, throw yourself into the sea,' and does not doubt in his heart but believes that what he says will happen, it will be done for him. Therefore I tell you, whatever you ask for in prayer, believe that you have received it, and it will be yours"* (Mark 11:23-24).

For *"God is not a man, that he should lie, nor a son of man, that he should change his mind"* (Numbers 23:19), as promised God indeed answers to the prayer of all those who believe and ask for His glory. People who love God and possess faith are bound to believe and seek for God's glory and that is why they are told to ask for whatever they wish. As they believe, ask, and receive answers to whatever they ask, these people can give glory to God. Let us rid ourselves of doubts but only believe, ask, and receive from God so that we can give glory to Him to our hearts' content.

Destroy the Wall of Sin of Not Sowing Before God

As the Governor of everything in the universe, God has established the law of the spiritual realm and as a righteous Judge He guides everything in an orderly fashion.

King Darius could not rescue his beloved servant Daniel from the lions' den because, even as king, he could not disobey the decree which he himself had put in writing. Likewise, for God cannot disobey the law of the spiritual realm *He Himself* has established, everything in the universe is run systematically under His supervision. Therefore, "God is not mocked" and allows a man to reap whatever he sows (Galatians 6:7). If one sows prayer, he receives spiritual blessings; if he sows his time, he receives the blessings of good health; if he sows offerings, God keeps him away from troubles at his business, work, and home, and gives even greater material blessings.

When we sow before God in various ways, He answers our prayer and gives us whatever we ask. By zealously sowing before God, let us not only bear abundant fruit but also receive whatever we ask Him in prayer.

In addition to the six walls of sin mentioned above, "sin" includes such desires and works of the flesh as unrighteousness, envy, rage, anger, and pride, not fighting against sins to the point of shedding blood and not being zealous for the kingdom of God. By learning and understanding a variety of factors that constitute a wall standing between God and us, let us destroy the wall of sin and always receive God's answers, thereby giving glory to Him. All of us ought to become believers who enjoy good health and have our every affair go well even as our souls prosper.

Based on God's Word found in Isaiah 59:1-2, we have examined a number of factors that constitute a wall standing between God and us. May each of you become God's blessed child who first understands the nature of this wall, enjoys good health and has his every affair succeed even as his soul prospers, and gives glory to his heavenly Father by receiving everything for which he asks in prayer, in the name of Jesus Christ I pray!

Chapter 5

You Reap What You Have Sowed

2 Corinthians 9:6-7

"Now this I say, he who sows sparingly will also reap sparingly, and he who sows bountifully will also reap bountifully. Each one must do just as he has purposed in his heart, not grudgingly or under compulsion, for God loves a cheerful giver."

Every autumn, we can see the abundance of golden waves of ripe rice plants in the field. For these rice plants to be harvested, we know there have been farmers' toil and dedication from planting of seeds to fertilizing of the field to nurturing the plants throughout the spring and summer.

A farmer who has a large field and sow more seeds must toil more than a farmer who sows less seeds. But in hopes of harvesting a large crop he works more diligently and arduously. Just as the law of nature dictates that "One reaps what he has sowed," we ought to know that the law of God who is the Owner of the spiritual realm follows the same pattern.

Among today's Christians, some keep asking God to fulfill their desires without sowing while others complain about the lack of His answers despite much prayer. Although God wants to give His children overflowing blessings and give answers to each of their problems, man often fails to understand the law of sowing and reaping and thus does not receive what he desires from God.

Based on the law of nature that tells us, "One reaps what he has sowed," let us find out what we are to sow and how we are to sow them in order to always receive God's answers and give glory to Him without reservation.

The Field Must First Be Cultivated

Before sowing seeds, a farmer must cultivate the field in which he is to work. He picks out stones, levels the ground, and creates an environment and condition in which the seeds can grow properly. According to the farmer's dedication and toil, even a desolate land can be turned into fertile soil.

The Bible likens the heart of each person to a field and categorizes it into four different types (Matthew 13:3-9).

The first type is "a field beside the road."

The soil of the field along the road is solid. An individual of such a heart does attend church but even after hearing the Word, he does not open the door to his heart. Therefore, he is unable to know God and, due to the lack of faith, fails to become enlightened.

The second type is "a rocky field."

In that rocky field, because of the stones in the field, buds cannot grow properly. An individual of such a heart knows the Word merely as knowledge and his faith is not accompanied by deed. For he lacks the certainty of faith, he falls quickly in times of trial and suffering.

The third type is "a thorny field."

In that thorny field, because thorns grow up and choke the plants, good fruits cannot be harvested. An individual of such a heart believes in God's Word and tries to live by it. But he does not act according to God's will but in accordance with the desires of the flesh. For the growth of the Word sown in his heart is tampered by temptation of property and profit or concerns of this world, he cannot bear fruit. Even though he prays, he is unable to rely on the "invisible" God and thus is quick to involve his own thoughts and ways. That is why he fails to experience God's power as He can only watch that person from afar.

The fourth type is "good soil."

A believer with this good field only says "Amen" to anything that is the Word of God and obeys it by faith without bringing in any of his thoughts or doing calculation. When seeds are sown in this good soil, they grow well and bear fruit a hundred, sixty or thirty times what has been sown.

Jesus only said "Amen" and was faithful to the Word of God (Philippians 2:5-8). Likewise, an individual of a "good soil" heart is unconditionally faithful to God's Word and lives by it. If His Word tells him to be joyful always, he is joyful in all circumstances. If His Word tells him to pray continually, he prays incessantly. A person who possesses a "good soil" heart can always communicate with God, receive whatever he asks in prayer, and live by His will.

No matter what kind of field we may have at the time being, we can always turn it into good soil. We can plow up stony fields and pick out stones, remove thorns, and fertilize any fields.

How then can we cultivate our hearts into "good soil"?

First, we are to worship God in spirit and in truth.
We must give God all our mind, will, dedication, and strength, and in love offer Him our heart. Only then will we be kept safe from idle thoughts, fatigue, and drowsiness and be able to turn our hearts into good soil by the power that comes from above.

Second, we must discard our sins to the point of shedding blood.
As we fully obey all of God's Word, including all the "Do this" and "Don't do that" commands, and live by it, our heart will gradually turn into good soil. For instance, when envy, jealousy, hatred and the like are discovered, only by fervent prayer can our heart turn into good soil.

As much as we examine the field of our heart and diligently cultivate it, our faith grows all the more and in God's love our every affair goes well. We must zealously cultivate our land because the more we live by God's Word, the more our spiritual faith grows. The more our spiritual faith grows, the more "good soil" we can possess. For this we must cultivate our heart all the more diligently.

Different Seeds Must Be Sown

Once the land has been cultivated, the farmer begins to sow seeds. Just as we ingest different types of food in balance to maintain our health, the farmer plants and grows such different seeds as rice, wheat, vegetables, beans, and the like.

In sowing before God, we are to sow many different things. "Sowing" spiritually refers to obeying, among God's commands, what He tells us to "Do." For instance, if God tells us to rejoice always, we can sow with our joy which stems from our hopes for Heaven, and by this joy God is also delighted and He gives us the desires of our heart (Psalm 37:4). If He tells us to "Preach the gospel," we must diligently spread God's Word. If He tells us to "Love one another," "Be faithful," "Be thankful," and "Pray," we ought to do exactly and diligently what we have been told.

In addition, for living by God's Word such as giving tithes and keeping the Sabbath holy is an act of sowing before Him, what we sow can bud, grow well, bloom, and bear abundant fruit.

If we sow sparingly, reluctantly, or under compulsion, God does not accept our effort. Just as a farmer sows his seeds in hopes of a good harvest in the fall, by faith we must also believe in and fix our eyes on God who blesses us a hundred, sixty, or thirty times what we sow.

Hebrews 11:6 tells us, *"And without faith it is impossible to please Him, for he who comes to God must believe that He is and that He is a rewarder of those who seek Him."* Putting our trust in His Word, when we look to our God who rewards and sow before Him, we can reap abundantly in this world and store our rewards in the heavenly kingdom.

The Field Must Be Tended in Perseverance and with Dedication

After sowing seeds, the farmer tends the field with utmost care. He waters the plants, weeds it, and catches any bugs. Without such persevering efforts, plants may spring up but wither and die before bearing any fruit.

Spiritually, "water" stands for God's Word. As Jesus tells us in John 4:14, *"But whoever drinks of the water that I will give him shall never thirst; but the water that I will give him will become in him a well of water springing up to eternal life,"* water symbolizes eternal life and the truth. "Catching of bugs" stands for keeping guard of God's Word planted in our heart field against the enemy devil. Through worship, praise, and prayer fullness in our heart can be maintained even if the enemy devil comes to interfere with our fieldwork.

"Weeding of the field" is the process in which we discard such untruths as rage, hatred, and the like. As we pray diligently and strive to throw away rage and hatred, rage is rooted out as a seed of meekness springs up and hatred is rooted out as a seed of love springs up. When the untruths have been weeded and the interfering enemy devil has been caught, we can grow up as His true children. An important factor in tending the field after having sown seeds is waiting for the right time in perseverance. If the farmer digs up the ground soon after sowing the seeds to see whether or not his plants are springing up, the seeds can rot easily. Until harvest, a great deal of dedication and perseverance is required.

The time necessary to bear fruit differs from seed to seed. While melon or watermelon seeds can bear fruit in less than a year, apple and pear trees need a few years. A ginseng farmer's joy would be exceedingly greater than that of a watermelon farmer, as the value of ginseng that has been cultivated for years cannot be compared to that of watermelons, which have been grown for a shorter amount of time.

By the same token, when we sow before God according to His Word, sometimes we may be able to receive His answers right away and harvest the fruit but at other times, more time may be required. As Galatians 6:9 reminds us, *"Let us not lose heart in doing good, for in due time we will reap if we do not grow weary,"* until the time of harvest we must tend our field in perseverance and with dedication.

You Reap What You Have Sowed

In John 12:24 Jesus tells us, *"Truly, truly, I say to you, unless a grain of wheat falls into the earth and dies, it remains alone; but if it dies, it bears much fruit."* According to His law, the

God of justice planted Jesus Christ His only begotten Son as an atoning sacrifice of mankind and allowed Him to become a kernel of wheat, fall, and die. Through His death, Jesus produced many fruit.

The law of the spiritual realm is, similar to the law of nature that dictates "You reap what you sow," the law of God which cannot be violated. Galatians 6:7-8 explicitly tells us, *"Do not be deceived, God is not mocked; for whatever a man sows, this he will also reap. For the one who sows to his own flesh will from the flesh reap corruption, but the one who sows to the Spirit will from the Spirit reap eternal life."*

When a farmer sows seeds in his field, depending on the kinds of seed, he may harvest some crops earlier than others and continues to sow seeds as he reaps. The more the farmer sows and diligently tends his field, the greater a crop he will harvest. By the same token, even in our relationship with God we reap what we sow.

If you sow prayer and praise, by the power from above you can live by God's Word as your soul prospers. If you faithfully work for the kingdom of God, any diseases will leave you as you receive the blessings in flesh and spirit. If you zealously sow with your material possessions, tithes, and thanksgiving offerings, He will give you greater material blessings by which He enables you to use them for His kingdom and righteousness.

Our Lord, who rewards each person according to what he has done, tells us in John 5:29, *"Those who did the good deeds [will come forth] to a resurrection of life, those who committed the evil deeds to a resurrection of judgment."* Thus, we must live by the Holy Spirit and do good in our lives.

If one sows not for the Holy Spirit but for his own desires, he can only reap things of this world that are to eventually pass away. If you measure and judge others, you will also be measured and judged according to God's Word saying that *"Do not judge so that you will not be judged. For in the way you judge, you will be judged; and by your standard of measure, it will be measured to you"* (Matthew 7:1-2).

God forgave us of all our sins we committed before we accepted Jesus Christ. But if we commit sins after knowing the truth and about sin, even if we are forgiven by repenting, we will receive retribution.

If you have sown sin, according to the law of the spiritual realm, you will reap the fruit of your sin and face times of trial and suffering.

When God's beloved David sinned, God said to him, *"Why have you despised the word of the LORD by doing evil in His sight?"* and *"Behold, I will raise up adversity against you from your own house"* (2 Samuel 12:9; 11). While David was forgiven of his sins when he repented, "I have sinned against the LORD," we also know that God struck the child that Uriah's wife had borne to David (2 Samuel 12:13-15).

We ought to live by the truth and do good, remember that we reap what we sow in everything, sow for the Holy Spirit, receive eternal life from the Holy Spirit, and always receive God's overflowing blessings.

In the Bible are many individuals who pleased God and subsequently received His abundant blessings. For the woman in Shunem had always treated Elisha the man of God with utmost respect and courtesy, he stayed at her house whenever he came by the area. After she discussed with her husband about preparing a guest room for Elisha, the woman set up a room for the prophet and placed a bed, a table, a chair, and a lamp and urged Elisha to stay at her house (2 Kings 4:8-10).

Elisha was greatly moved by the woman's devotion. When he found out that her husband was old and they were childless, and that having a child of her own was the woman's wish, Elisha asked God for the blessing of birth for this woman, and God gave her a son a year later (2 Kings 4:11-17).

As God promises us in Psalm 37:4, *"Delight yourself in the LORD; and He will give you the desires of your heart,"* the woman in Shunem was given the desires of her heart as she treated God's servant with care and dedication (2 Kings 4:8-17).

In Acts 9:36-40 is a record of a woman in Joppa named Tabitha, who abounded with deeds of kindness and charity. When she became ill and died, the disciples reported the news to Peter. When he arrived at the scene, the widows there showed Peter the robes and other clothing Tabitha had made for them, and begged him to bring the woman back to life. Peter was deeply moved by the women's gesture and earnestly prayed to God. When he said, "Tabitha, get up," she opened her eyes and sat up. For Tabitha had sown before God by doing good and helping the poor, she could receive the blessing of the extension of her life.

In Mark 12:44 is a record of a poor widow who gave God her everything. Jesus, who watched the crowd giving offerings at the temple, said to His disciples, *"For they all put in out of their surplus, but she, out of her poverty, put in all she owned, all she had to live on"* and commended her. It is not difficult to know that the woman received greater blessings later on in her life.

According to the law of the spiritual realm, the God of justice allows us to reap what we sow and rewards us according to what each of us has done. For God works according to each individual's faith as he believes in His Word and obeys it, we ought to understand that we can receive anything we ask in prayer. With this in mind, may each of you examine your heart, diligently cultivate it into good soil, sow many seeds, tend them in perseverance and with dedication, and bear abundant fruit, in the name of our Lord Jesus Christ I pray!

Chapter 6

Elijah Receives God's Answer by Fire

1 Kings 18:41-45

Now Elijah said to Ahab, "Go up, eat and drink; for there is the sound of the roar of a heavy shower." So Ahab went up to eat and drink. But Elijah went up to the top of Carmel; and he crouched down on the earth and put his face between his knees. He said to his servant, "Go up now, look toward the sea." So he went up and looked and said, "There is nothing." And he said, "Go back" seven times. It came about at the seventh time, that he said, "Behold, a cloud as small as a man's hand is coming up from the sea." And he said, "Go up, say to Ahab, 'Prepare your chariot and go down, so that the heavy shower does not stop you.'" In a little while the sky grew black with clouds and wind, and there was a heavy shower. And Ahab rode and went to Jezreel.

The powerful servant of God Elijah could testify to the living God and make possible for the idol-worshiping Israelites to repent of their sins with God's answer by fire he asked and received. In addition, when there had been no rain for three and a half years because of God's anger against the Israelites, it was Elijah who performed the miracle of ending the drought and bringing down a heavy rain.

If we believe in the living God, in our lives we must also receive God's answer by fire like Elijah, testify to Him, and give glory to Him.

By exploring Elijah's faith, by which he received God's answer *by fire* and saw with his own eyes the fulfillment of the desires of his heart, let us also become God's blessed children who always receive our Father's answers by fire.

The Faith of Elijah, the Servant of God

As God's elect, the Israelites had to worship God alone, but their kings began doing evil in God's sight and worshiping idols. By the time Ahab ascended to the throne, the people of Israel began doing more evil and the idol-worshiping reached its culmination. At this point, God's anger against Israel turned into the calamity of three-and-a-half-year drought. God established Elijah as His servant and through him manifested His works.

God told Elijah, *"Go, show yourself to Ahab, and I will send rain on the face of the earth"* (1 Kings 18:1).

Moses, who brought the Israelites out of Egypt, at first disobeyed God when He commanded Moses to go before Pharaoh. When Samuel was told to anoint David, the prophet initially disobeyed God as well. However, when God told Elijah to go and show himself to Ahab, the very king who had been trying to kill him for three years, this prophet unconditionally obeyed God and showed Him the kind of faith with which God was pleased.

For Elijah obeyed and believed in everything that was God's Word, through the prophet God could manifest His works again and again. God was pleased with Elijah's obedient faith, loved him, recognized him as His servant, accompanied him wherever he went, and guaranteed his every endeavor. For God certified Elijah's faith, he could raise the dead, receive God's answer by fire, and be taken up to Heaven in a whirlwind. Although there is only one God who is seated in His heavenly throne, the almighty God can oversee everything in the universe and allow His work to take place wherever He is present. As we find in Mark 16:20, *"And they went out and preached everywhere, while the Lord worked with them, and confirmed the word by the signs that followed,"* when an individual and his faith are recognized and certified by God, miracles and His answers to the person's prayer are accompanied as a token of the manifestations of His work.

Elijah Receives God's Answer by Fire

For Elijah's faith was great and he was obedient enough to be worthy of God's recognition, the prophet could boldly prophesy about the impending drought in Israel.

He could proclaim to Ahab the king, *"As the LORD, the God of Israel lives, before whom I stand, surely there shall be neither dew nor rain these years, except by my word"* (1 Kings 17:1).

For God already knew that Ahab would endanger the life of Elijah who prophesied about the drought, God led the prophet to the brook Cherith, told him to stay there a while, and ordered the ravens to bring him bread and meat in the morning and in the evening. When the brook Cherith dried up from the lack of rain, God led Elijah to Zarephath and let a widow there supply him with food.

When the widow's son became ill, grew worse and worse, and eventually died, Elijah called out to God in prayer: *"O LORD my God, I pray You, let this child's life return to him"* (1 Kings 17:21).

God heard Elijah's prayer, brought the boy back to life, and allowed him to live. Through this incident, God proved that Elijah was a man of God and that the Word of God in his mouth is the truth (1 Kings 17:24).

People of our generation live in a time when they can never believe God unless they see miraculous signs and wonders (John 4:48). In order to testify to the living God today, each of us must be armed with the kind of faith Elijah possessed and take charge in boldly spreading the gospel.

In the third year of the prophecy in which Elijah said to Ahab, *"Surely there shall be neither dew nor rain these years, except by my word,"* God told His prophet, *"Go, show yourself to Ahab, and I will send rain on the face of the earth"* (1 Kings 18:1). We find in Luke 4:25 that *"in the days of Elijah, when the sky was shut up for three years and six months, when a great famine came over all the land."* In other words, there was no rain in Israel for three and a half years. Before Elijah went to Ahab the second time, the king had searched in vain for the prophet even in neighboring countries, believing that Elijah was to blame for the three-and-a-half-year drought.

Even though Elijah would have been put to death the moment he went before Ahab, he boldly obeyed God's Word. When Elijah stood before Ahab, the king asked him, *"Is this you, you troubler of Israel?"* (1 Kings 18:17) To this Elijah responded, *"I have not troubled Israel, but you and your father's house have, because you have forsaken the commandments of the LORD and you have followed the Baals"* (1 Kings 18:18). He conveyed to the king God's will, and never feared. Elijah took one step further and said to Ahab, *"Now then send and gather to me all Israel at Mount Carmel, together with 450 prophets of Baal and 400 prophets of the Asherah, who eat at Jezebel's table"* (1 Kings 18:19).

For Elijah was well aware that the drought came upon Israel

because of its people's idol-worshiping, he sought to contend with 850 prophets of idols and affirmed, "The God who answers by fire – He is God." For Elijah believed in God, the prophet showed Him the faith by which he believed that God would answer by fire.

He then said to Baal's prophets, *"Choose one ox for yourselves and prepare it first for you are many, and call on the name of your god, but put no fire under it"* (1 Kings 18:25). When Baal's prophets did not receive any answer from the morning to the evening, Elijah taunted them.

Elijah believed God would answer him by fire, in gladness ordered the Israelites to build the altar and pour water over the offering and on the wood, and prayed to God.

Answer me, O LORD, answer me, that this people may know that You, O LORD, are God, and that You have turned their heart back again (1 Kings 18:37).

At this, the fire of the LORD fell and consumed the burnt offering and the wood and the stones and the dust, and licked up the water that was in the trench. When all the people saw it, they fell on their faces; and they said, *"The LORD, He is God; the LORD, He is God"* (1 Kings 18:38-39).

All this was made possible because Elijah did not doubt even a little when he asked God (James 1:6) and believed that he already received what he had asked for in prayer (Mark 11:24).

Why did Elijah order water to be poured over the offering

and then pray? For the drought had lasted three and a half years, the scarcest and most valuable of all necessities at the time was water. By filling four large jars with water and pouring the water on the offering *three* times (1 Kings 18:33-34), Elijah showed God his faith and gave Him what was the most precious to him. God who loves a cheerful giver (2 Corinthians 9:7) not only allowed Elijah to reap what he had sown, but also gave the prophet His answer by fire and proved to all Israelites their God was indeed alive.

As we follow Elijah's footsteps and show God our faith, give Him our most precious thing, and prepare ourselves to receive His answers to our prayer, we can testify the living God to all people with His answers by fire.

Elijah Brings Down a Heavy Rain

After presenting the living God to the Israelites through His answer by fire and making the idol-worshiping Israelites repent, Elijah remembered the oath he had made to Ahab -*"As the LORD, the God of Israel lives, before whom I stand, surely there shall be neither dew nor rain these years, except by my word"* (1 Kings 17:1). He said to the king, *"Go up, eat and drink; for there is the sound of the roar of a heavy shower"* (1 Kings 18:42), and went up to the top of Carmel. He did so in order to fulfill God's Word, *"I will send rain on the face of the earth,"* (1 Kings 18:1) and receive His answer.

Once at the top of Carmel, Elijah crouched down on the earth and put his face between his knees. Why did Elijah pray in such a manner? Elijah was in so much anguish while he prayed.

Through this image, we can presume how earnestly Elijah called out to God with all his heart. Moreover, until he could see God's answer with his own eyes, Elijah did not stop praying. The prophet instructed his servant to keep his eyes toward the sea and until the servant saw a cloud as small as a man's hand, Elijah prayed in this manner seven times. This was more than enough to impress God and shake His heavenly throne. For Elijah brought down a rain after three and a half years of drought, it can be presumed that his prayer was exceedingly powerful.

When Elijah received God's answer by fire, he acknowledged with his lips that God would work for him even though God had not spoken of it; he did the same when he brought down the rain. Upon seeing a cloud as small as a man's hand, the prophet sent a word to Ahab, *"Prepare your chariot and go down, so that the heavy shower does not stop you"* (1 Kings 18:44). For Elijah had the faith by which he could acknowledge with his lips even if he could not yet see (Hebrews 11:1), God could work according to the prophet's faith, and indeed according to Elijah's faith, in a little while the sky grew black with clouds and wind, and there was a heavy shower (1 Kings 18:45).

We must believe that the God, who gave Elijah His answer by fire and a long-awaited rain after a drought that had lasted three years and six months, is the same God who drives away our trials and sufferings, gives us the desires of our heart, and gives us His wondrous blessings.

By now, I am sure you have realized that in order to receive God's answer by fire, give glory to Him, and fulfill the desires of your heart, you must first show Him the kind of faith with which He will be pleased, destroy any wall of sin that stands between God and you, and ask Him for anything without doubting.

Second, in gladness you must build an altar before God, give Him offerings, and pray earnestly. Third, until you receive His answers, you are to acknowledge with your lips God will work for you. God will then be greatly pleased and answer your prayer in order for you to give glory to Him to your heart's content.

Our God answers us when we pray to Him with problems concerning our souls, children, health, job, or any other matters, and receives the glory from us. Let us also possess whole faith like that of Elijah, pray until we receive God's answers, and become His blessed children, always giving glory to our Father!

Chapter 7

How to Fulfill the Desires of Your Heart

Psalm 37:4

"Delight yourself in the LORD; and He will give you the desires of your heart."

Many people today seek to receive answers to a variety of problems from the almighty God. They zealously pray, fast, and pray through the night to receive healing, rebuild their failed businesses, give birth to children, and receive material blessings. Unfortunately, there are more people who are unable to receive God's answers and give glory to Him than those who are able.

When they do not hear from God in a month or two months' time, these people grow weary, saying, "God doesn't exist," turn away from God altogether, and begin worshipping idols, thereby tarnishing His name. If a person does attend church but fails to receive God's power and give glory to Him, how could this be "true faith"?

If one professes to truly believe in God, then as His child, he must be able to receive the desires of his heart and fulfill whatever he seeks to accomplish during his life in this world. But many fail to fulfill the desires of their heart even if they proclaim to believe. It is because they do not know themselves. With the passage on which this chapter is based, let us explore the ways in which we could accomplish the desires of our heart.

First, One Must Examine His Own Heart

Each individual must look back and see whether he truly believes in the almighty God, or only believes half-heartedly while doubting, or is of a cunning heart who only seeks some kind of luck. Before coming to know Jesus Christ, most people spend their life either worshiping idols or trusting only themselves. In times of a major trial or suffering, however, after realizing that the disasters they face cannot be resolved by the might of man or their idols, they wonder about the world, hear along the way that God can solve their problems, and end up coming before Him.

Instead of fixing their eyes on the God of power, the people of this world merely think in doubt, 'Wouldn't He answer me if I begged Him?' or 'Well, maybe prayer could solve my crisis.' Yet, the almighty God governs the history of mankind as well as man's life, death, curse, and blessing, revives the dead, and searches man's heart, so He does not answer an individual with a doubting heart (James 1:6-8).

If one truly seeks to fulfill the desires of his heart, he must first throw away his doubting and luck-seeking heart, and believe that he has already received everything he asks the almighty God in prayer. Only then will the God of power bestow His love and allow him to fulfill the desires of his heart.

Second, One's Assurance of Salvation and Condition of Faith Must Be Examined

At church today, many believers are subject to problems in their faith. It is very heartbreaking to see a surprisingly large number of people who are wandering spiritually, those who fail to see, because of their spiritual arrogance, that their faith is headed in the wrong direction, and others who lack the assurance of salvation even after many years of life in Christ and service for Him.

Romans 10:10 tells us, *"For with the heart a person believes, resulting in righteousness, and with the mouth he confesses, resulting in salvation."* When you open the door to your heart and accept Jesus Christ as your Savior, by the grace of the Holy Spirit that is given freely from above, you receive the authority as a child of God. Furthermore, when you confess with your lips that Jesus Christ is your Savior and believe from your heart that God has raised Jesus from the dead, you will become certain of your salvation.

If you do not know for sure whether or not you have received salvation, there is a problem with the condition of your faith. This is because, if you lack the certainty of God's being your Father and your having attained heavenly citizenship and become His child, you cannot live by the Father's will.

For this reason, Jesus tells us, *"Not everyone who says to Me, 'Lord, Lord,' will enter the kingdom of heaven, but he who does the will of My Father who is in heaven will enter"* (Matthew 7:21). If the "God the Father-son (or daughter)" relationship has not yet come into being to an individual, it is only natural for that person not to receive His answers. Even if that relationship has taken form, however, if there is something wrong in his heart in the sight of God, he cannot receive God's answers, either.

Therefore, if you become God's child who has the assurance

of salvation and repent of not living by the will of God, He resolves every one of your problems including disease, failure of business, and financial trouble, and in all things He works for your good.

If you seek God for the problem you have with your child, with the Word of the truth God helps you to figure out any problems and issues that exist between yourself and your child. At times, the children are to blame; more often, however, it is parents who are responsible for the difficulty with their children. Before starting finger-pointing, if parents themselves first turn from their erroneous ways and repent of them, strive to raise their children properly, and commit everything to God, He gives them wisdom and works for the good of both parents and their children.

Therefore, if you come to church and seek to receive answers to the trouble with your children, disease, finance, and the like, instead of hastily fasting, praying, or staying up all night in prayer, you must first figure out by the truth what has clogged the channel between you and God, repent, and turn away. God will then work for your good as you receive the guidance of the Holy Spirit. If you do not even try to understand, hear the Word of God, or live by it, your prayer will not bring you God's answers.

For there are many instances in which people fail to wholly grasp the truth and fail to receive God's answers and blessings, all of us must fulfill the desires of our heart by becoming sure of our salvation and living by God's will (Deuteronomy 28:1-14).

Third, You Must Please God with Your Deeds

If anyone acknowledges God the Creator and accepts Jesus Christ as his Savior, as much as he learns the truth and becomes enlightened, his soul prospers. In addition, as he continues to discover the heart of God, he can live his life in a way that is pleasing to Him. While two- or three-year-old toddlers do not know ways to please their parents, in their adolescence and adulthood the children learn to delight them. By the same token, the more God's children comprehend and live by the truth, the greater they can please their Father.

Again and again, the Bible tells us of the ways in which our forefathers in faith received answers to their prayer by pleasing God. How did Abraham please God?

Abraham always sought and lived in peace and holiness (Genesis 13:9), served God with all his body, heart, and mind (Genesis 18:1-10), and wholly obeyed Him without involving his own thoughts (Hebrews 11:19; Genesis 22:12), because he believed that God could raise the dead. As a result, Abraham received the blessing of Jehovahjireh or "The LORD Will Provide," the blessing of children, the blessing of finance, the blessing of good health, and the like, and blessings in every way (Genesis 22:16-18, 24:1).

What did Noah do to receive God's blessings? He was righteous, blameless among the people of his generation, and walked with God (Genesis 6:9). When the judgment of water submerged the whole world, only Noah and his family could avoid the judgment and receive salvation. For Noah walked with God, he could heed God's voice and prepare an ark and lead even his family to salvation.

When the widow in Zarephath in 1 Kings 17:8-16 planted a seed of faith in God's servant Elijah during a three-and-a-half-year drought in Israel, she received extraordinary blessings. As she obeyed in faith and served Elijah with bread made from only a handful of flour in the bowl and a little oil in the jar, God blessed her and fulfilled His prophetic Word saying that *"The bowl of flour shall not be exhausted, nor shall the jar of oil be empty, until the day that the LORD sends rain on the face of the earth"* (v. 14).

For the woman in Shunem in 2 Kings 4:8-17 served and treated God's servant Elisha with utmost care and respect, she received the blessing of giving birth to a son. The woman served God's servant not because she wanted something in return, but because she earnestly loved God from her heart. Does it not make sense for this woman to have received God's blessing?

It is also easy to tell that God must have been thoroughly delighted with the faith of Daniel and his three friends. Even though Daniel was thrown into the lions' den for having prayed to God, he walked out of the den without any wound because he trusted God (Daniel 6:16-23). Even though Daniel's three friends were bound and thrown into the burning furnace for not having worshiped an idol, they gave glory to God after walking out of the furnace without any of their body parts burned or even singed (Daniel 3:19-26).

The centurion in Matthew 8 could please God with his great faith and, according to his faith, received God's answers. When he told Jesus that his servant was paralyzed and in terrible suffering, Jesus offered to visit the centurion's house and heal his servant. Yet, when the centurion said to Jesus, *"Just say the word, and my servant will be healed,"* (v. 8) and showed his great faith and great love for his servant, Jesus commended him, *"I have not found such great faith with anyone in Israel"* (v. 10). For one receives God's answers according to his faith, the centurion's servant was healed that very moment. Hallelujah!

There are more. In Mark 5:25-34 we see the faith of a woman who had been suffering from bleeding for 12 years. Despite the care of many doctors and the money she spent, her condition kept growing worse. When she heard news about Jesus, the woman believed she could be healed only if she touched His clothes. When she came up behind Jesus and touched His cloak, the woman was healed at that very moment.

What kind of heart did a centurion named Cornelius in Acts 10:1-8 possess and in what ways did he, a Gentile, serve God that all his family received salvation? We find that Cornelius and all family were devout and God-fearing; and he gave generously to those in need and prayed to God regularly. Therefore, Cornelius' prayers and gifts to the poor had come up as a memorial offering before God and as Peter visited his house to worship God, everyone in Cornelius' family received the Holy Spirit and began speaking in tongues.

In Acts 9:36-42 we find a woman named Tabitha (which, when translated, is Dorcas) who had always done good and helped the poor, but became ill and died. When Peter came at the urging of the disciples, got down on his knees, and prayed, Tabitha came back to life.

When His children carry out their duties and please their Father, the living God fulfills the desires of their heart and in all things works for their good. When we can truly believe in this fact, throughout our lives we will always receive God's answers.

Through consultations or dialogues from time to time, I hear of people who once had great faith, served the church well, and were faithful, but abandoned God after a period of trial and suffering. Each time, I cannot help feeling brokenhearted for people's inability to make spiritual distinction.

If people have true faith, they will not abandon God even when a trial comes their way. If they have spiritual faith, they will be joyful, grateful, and praying even in times of trial and suffering. They will not betray God, be tempted, or miss their footing in Him. Sometimes people can be faithful in hopes of receiving blessings or to be recognized by others. But the prayer of faith and the prayer full of hopes of fortuity can easily be distinguished by their respective results. If one prays by spiritual faith, his prayer will most certainly be accompanied by deeds that are pleasing to God, and he will give great glory to Him by fulfilling the desires of his heart one by one.

With the Bible as our guide, we have examined how our forefathers in faith showed their faith to God and with what kind of heart they could please Him and fulfill the desires of their heart. For God blesses, as promised, all those who please Him–the way Tabitha who was brought back to life pleased Him, the way the childless woman in Shunem who was blessed with a son pleased Him, and the way the woman who was freed from 12 years of bleeding pleased Him–let us believe and set our eyes on Him.

God says to us, *"'If You can?' All things are possible to him who believes"* (Mark 9:23). When we believe that He can put an end to any of our problems, wholly commit to Him all the problems concerning our faith, diseases, children, and finance and rely on Him, He will surely take care of all this for us (Psalm 37:5).

By pleasing God who does not lie but carries out what He has spoken, may each of you fulfill the desires of your heart, give great glory to God, and lead a blessed life, in the name of Jesus Christ I pray!

The Author
Dr. Jaerock Lee

Dr. Jaerock Lee was born in Muan, Jeonnam Province, Republic of Korea, in 1943. In his twenties, Dr. Lee suffered from a variety of incurable diseases for seven years and awaited death with no hope for recovery. One day in the spring of 1974, however, he was led to a church by his sister and when he knelt down to pray, the living God immediately healed him of all his diseases.

From the moment Dr. Lee met the living God through that wonderful experience, he has loved God with all his heart and sincerity, and in 1978 he was called to be a servant of God. He prayed fervently with countless fasting prayers so that he could clearly understand the will of God, wholly accomplish it and obey the Word of God. In 1982, he founded Manmin Central Church in Seoul, Korea, and countless works of God, including miraculous healings and wonders, have been taking place at his church.

In 1986, Dr. Lee was ordained as a pastor at the Annual Assembly of Jesus' Sungkyul Church of Korea, and four years later in 1990, his sermons began to be broadcast in Australia, Russia, the Philippines, and many more through the Far East Broadcasting Company, the Asia Broadcast Station, and the Washington Christian Radio System.

Three years later in 1993, Manmin Central Church was selected as one of the "World's Top 50 Churches" by the *Christian World* magazine (US) and he received an Honorary Doctorate of Divinity from Christian Faith College, Florida, USA, and in 1996 a Ph. D. in Ministry from Kingsway Theological Seminary, Iowa, USA.

Since 1993, Dr. Lee has taken the lead in world mission through many overseas crusades in Tanzania, Argentina, L.A., Baltimore City, Hawaii, and New York City of the USA, Uganda, Japan, Pakistan, Kenya, the Philippines, Honduras, India, Russia, Germany, Peru, Democratic Republic of the Congo, Israel and Estonia. In 2002 he was called a "worldwide revivalist" by major Christian newspapers in Korea for his powerful ministry work in various overseas Great United Crusades, his 'New York Crusade 2006' held in Madison Square Garden, the most world-famous arena, was broadcast to 220 nations, and in the Israel United Crusade 2009 held in International Convention Center in Jerusalem he boldly proclaimed Jesus Christ is the Messiah and Savior.

As of August of 2011, Manmin Central Church has a congregation of more than 120,000 members. There are 9,000 branch churches throughout the globe including 54 domestic branch churches, and so far more than 137 missionaries have been commissioned to 23 countries, including the United States, Russia, Germany, Canada, Japan, China, France, India, Kenya, and many more.

As of the date of this publishing, Dr. Lee has written 63 books, including bestsellers *Tasting Eternal Life before Death, My Life My Faith I & II, The Message of the Cross, The Measure of Faith, Heaven I & II, Hell,* and *The Power of God.* His works have been translated into more than 67 languages.

His Christian columns appear on *The Hankook Ilbo, The JoongAng Daily, The Chosun Ilbo, The Dong-A Ilbo, The Munhwa Ilbo, The Seoul Shinmun, The Kyunghyang Shinmun, The Hankyoreh Shinmun, The Korea Economic Daily, The Korea Herald, The Shisa News,* and *The Christian Press.*

Dr. Lee is currently leader of many missionary organizations and associations: including Chairman, The United Holiness Church of Jesus Christ; President, Manmin World Mission; Permanent President, The World Christianity Revival Mission Association; Founder, Manmin TV; Founder & Board Chairman, Global Christian Network (GCN); Founder & Board Chairman, World Christian Doctors Network (WCDN); and Founder & Board Chairman, Manmin International Seminary (MIS).

Other powerful books by the same author

Heaven I & II

A detailed sketch of the gorgeous living environment the heavenly citizens enjoy and beautiful description of different levels of heavenly kingdoms.

The Message of the Cross

A powerful awakening message for all the people who are spiritually asleep In this book you will find the reason Jesus is the only Savior and the true love of God.

Hell

An earnest message to all mankind from God, who wishes not even one soul to fall into the depths of hell! You will discover the never-before-revealed account of the cruel reality of the Lower Grave and hell.

Tasting Eternal Life Before Death

A testimonial memoirs of Dr. Jaerock Lee, who was born gain and saved from the valley of death and has been leading an exemplary Christian life.

The Measure of Faith

What kind of a dwelling place, crown and reward are prepared for you in heaven? This book provides with wisdom and guidance for you to measure your faith and cultivate the best and most mature faith.

www.urimbooks.com

www.ingramcontent.com/pod-product-compliance
Lightning Source LLC
LaVergne TN
LVHW010405070526
838199LV00065B/5900